NEVER

NEVER

POEMS

Jorie Graham

ecco

An Imprint of HarperCollinsPublishers

HarperCollins books may be purchased for educational, business, or sales promotional use.
For information please write: Special Markets Department,
HarperCollins Publishers Inc., 10 East 53rd Street, New York, NY 10022.

FIRST EDITION

BOOK DESIGN BY FEARN CUTLER DE VICQ

Library of Congress Cataloging-in-Publication Data

Graham, Jorie, 1951-
Never : poems / Jorie Graham.—1st ed.
p. cm.
ISBN 0-06-008471-5 (hardcover)
I. Title

PS3557.R214 N38 2002
811'.54—dc21
2001051279

02 03 04 05 06 ❖/RRD 10 9 8 7 6 5 4 3 2 1

This book is for Emily

Grateful acknowledgment to the editors of the following magazines and journals in which these poems (sometimes in altered form, or with different titles) first appeared: *The New Yorker, Conjunctions, The Kenyon Review, Denver Quarterly, Fence, Jubilat, Harvard Magazine*, the *New York Times* (Op-Ed page), the *New York Times Magazine, Boston Review, Countermeasures, Seneca Review, London Review of Books, The Times Literary Supplement, Volt, The American Poetry Review*.

A few of the poems were printed, in different versions in some cases, in a fine-press limited edition titled *All Things*, from the University of Iowa's Center for the Book. My thanks to Shari deGraw and Brien Woods.

"Evolution" ("How old are you?") was written on commission for the *New York Times Magazine* in response to a survey of American public sentiment at the close of the millennium. My thanks to David Shipley.

"Gulls" also appeared in *The Best American Poetry 2000* (ed. Robert Hass).

Some of this work was written for the Environmental Protection Agency, for use in a collaboration with the sculpture of Beverly Pepper.

A number of these poems were written on commission for the National Millennium Survey Project, in conjunction with the College of Santa Fe. My thanks to the whole organization, and to Greg Glazner in particular.

My gratitude, as well, to Robert Whiting (in Todos Santos), and Lila Stine (in Chilmark).

CONTENTS

"How can I believe in that? Surely it cannot be?"

John Keats, 1818

(upon first viewing the scenery of the Lake District)

I

PRAYER

Over a dock railing, I watch the minnows, thousands, swirl

themselves, each a minuscule muscle, but also, without the

way to *create* current, making of their unison (turning, re-

infolding,

entering and exiting their own unison in unison) making of themselves a

visual current, one that cannot freight or sway by

minutest fractions the water's downdrafts and upswirls, the

dockside cycles of finally-arriving boat-wakes, there where

they hit deeper resistance, water that seems to burst into

itself (it has those layers), a real current though mostly

invisible sending into the visible (minnows) arrowing

motion that forces change—

this is freedom. This is the force of faith. Nobody gets

what they want. Never again are you the same. The longing

is to be pure. What you get is to be changed. More and more by

each glistening minute, through which infinity threads itself,

also oblivion, of course, the aftershocks of something

at sea. Here, hands full of sand, letting it sift through

in the wind, I look in and say take this, this is

what I have saved, take this, hurry. And if I listen

now? Listen, I was not saying anything. It was only

something I did. I could not choose words. I am free to go.

I cannot of course come back. Not to this. Never.

It is a ghost posed on my lips. Here: never.

AFTERWARDS

I am beneath the tree. To the right the river is melting the young sun.

And translucence itself, bare, bony, feeding and growing on the manifest,

frets in the small puddles of snowmelt sidewalks and frozen lawns hold up

full of sky.

From this eternity, where we do not resemble ourselves, where

resemblance is finally

beside (as the river is) the point,

and attention can no longer change the outcome of the gaze,

the ear too is finally sated, starlings starting up ladderings of chatter,

all at once all to the left,

invisible in the pruned-back

hawthorn, heard and heard again, and yet again

differently heard, but silting

the head with inwardness and making always a

dispersing but still

coalescing opening in the listener who

cannot *look* at them exactly,

since they are invisible inside the greens—though screeching-full in

syncopations of yellowest,

fine-thought, finespun

rivering of almost-knowables. "Gold" is too dark. "Featherwork"

too thick. When two

appear in flight, straight to the child-sized pond of

melted snow,

and thrash, dunk, rise, shake, rethrashing, reconfiguring through

reshufflings and resettlings the whole body of integrated

featherwork,

they shatter open the blue-and-tree-tip filled-up gaze of
                              the lawn's two pools,
breaking and ruffling all the crisp true sky we had seen living
                              down in that tasseled
earth. How shall we say this *happened?* Something inaudible
has ceased. Has gone back round to an other side
of which this side's access was [is] this width of sky
                              deep in
just-greening soil? We left the party without a word.
We did not change, but time changed us. It should be,
it seems, one or the other of us who is supposed to say—lest
there be nothing—*here we are*. It was supposed to become familiar
(this earth). It was to become "ours." Lest there be nothing?
Lest we reach down to touch our own reflection here?
Shouldn't depth come to sight and let it in, in the end, as the form
the farewell takes: representation: dead men:
lean forward and look in: the raggedness of where the openings
are: precision of the limbs upthrusting down to hell:
the gleaming *in*: so blue: and that it *has* a bottom: even a few clouds
                              if you keep
attending: and something that's an *edge-of*: and mind-cracks: and how the
                                   poem is
about that: that distant life: I carry it inside me but
can plant it into soil: so that it becomes impossible
to say that anything swayed
from *in* to *out*: then back to "is this mine, or yours?": the mind
seeks danger out: it reaches in, would touch: where the subject is emptying,
                                   war is:
morality play: preface: what there is to be thought: love:
begin with the world: let it be small enough.

PHILOSOPHER'S STONE

It's like this. There are quantities. There's on-

goingness—

no—there's an underneath. Over it we lay

time—actually more like takes and re-

takes by

the mind (eyes closed) then clickings of

its opening-out and the mind fills

with gazes—thousands over some visualizations—or some

places if you wish—I wish—a few or no gazes over some

(because somewhere there must be a meadow with just such

grasses

no gaze has touched)—(because it *is*

touch)—(and other places where millions have laid down

their mental waters in this manner). Above and

below our gaze, I don't know for sure—although I

believe there must be a truth—gravity lays,

is laid, in—like a color being washed over

the whole—a tint with a direction in it—

or rather a tint that places tiny arrowings,

or the sensation of pulling of being pulled over

all of the visualization—eyes open now—over

sky, blue, stonewall, vectoring grasses, three trees,

distance, close-up—all as if

being drawn-in without it affecting *how*.

If you open and close your eyes

there should be a difference, no, in the way

the thing seen *is*—in its weight?—and then

what the thinking has begun to make—which is

not the tint of gravity, nor the *was* of the ticking,

(what's not there if we leave

altogether for example)—because there is, on it, which we've

somehow

introduced, this wash which is duration, a very

sturdy though of course not touchable fabric, and because

we can creep along it—or simply

count lengths back—because because of it there *is* a "back"—

not a *back* on the field itself but a back to the

thinking—which *does* begin now to apprehend the edges of

skeletal diminuendos of glancings as they

ascend the manifest up towards its upper reaches—soil,

timothy, stone, manyness of stone, non-mortared

build-up of it—

mistings of just-above-stone where the

two of them meet, manifest, un-manifest [and how they

could not

know who was looking at them][and that I was from

another country][down to the very movement of my lips]

[show me a word I can use][and how all that you say

is taken from you, they take it, just like

that, it becomes smoke] smoke rising here as mist off the heavy

topmost stones

of the wall, raised so carefully up from the field,

to make this edge of precarious positionings,

that make the suddenly-green silence actually hold still, hold

up—a kind of trophy

to property, to the property of gravity—a waltz

of motions (fallings, tumblings) stilled—

a thing of number without a numbering—as if every

movement

of some gathering crowd's lips were, having uttered each one

their one

request, cast forth into manifestation—slightly round with

syllable then placed—a long wall of requests so carefully placed—

each almost pitiful with fear and desire—from each request the soil

scraped-off—

where it's dug-up—

from the wide field it now defines—the hole

filling back in on itself—as the self fills in on itself—a

collectivity—a

god making of himself many

creatures [in the cage there is food][outside only the great

circle called freedom][an empire which begins

with a set table] and I should like, now that the last washes of my gaze

let loose over the field, to say, of this peering,

it is the self—there—out to the outer reaches of

my hand, holding it out before me now, putting it into where

my breath begins to whitely manifest my difference to

night air: look: it is a law: the air

draws on itself the self's soft temperature:

it looks like rain: there is a beforehand: I brought

my life from it thus far: moments are attached.

The nets of the glance draw in. Some

admixture is caught. Some not. There is

impatience but not in the self alone. The open

has its own impatience. The edges fill with it

there where a voice is raised.

Anticipation pulls one way. Regret the other.

A smile can open or close the face. Blood

is almost touchable by sun. Footsteps bent the grass

a bit

to get us here. Looking behind
I see the lift in the bent weeds, I see in them
what cannot be conceived of—quite—I see *it* rise, erasing
path. As where a hand
clutches a wound, tightly, stanching the blood.
Why did we take this way? Where does this *going*
go? Maybe it can bend down now and shut its hand
over a stone. To toss it hard across the field. To have it
land somewhere. Exactly. Yes. Somebody
loves you. Elsewhere a people now is being forced
from home. Looking out, as dusk comes on,
no looking up or down anymore.
Everything taken in as stone by grass.
Does one know
what one likes. What one is like. What is a feeling
in the heart. What troubles
the soul. What troubles the jonquils nearest me
as the light, the cage of this,
goes out. What is it that can now
step *out*. And is the open door through me.
Beyond us now, close-in, nearby,
how near I cannot tell, around us, in us, near: the
sensation of beauty unseen; an owlet's

cry;

a cry from something closer to the ground that's uttered
twice and which I cannot name—although it
seems bright yellow in its pitch.

WOODS

O stubborn appetite: *I,* then *I,*

loping through the poem. Shall I do that again?

Can we put our finger on it?

These lines have my breathing in them, yes.

Also my body was here. Why try to disguise it.

In this morning of my year

that will never be given back.

Also those who will not give it back. Whoever they

                                        may be.

How quietly they do their job

over this page. How can I know when it's the

case—oh swagger of dwelling in place, in voice—

surely one of us understands the importance.

Understands? Shall I wave a "finished" copy at you

whispering do you wish to come for lunch.

Nor do I want to dwell on this.

I cannot, actually, dwell on this.

There is no home. One can stand out here

and gesture wildly, yes. One can say "finished"

and look *into* the woods, as I do now, here,

but also casting my eye out

to see (although that was yesterday)(in through the alleyways

of trees) the slantings of morninglight

(speckling)(golden) laying in

these foliate patternings, this goldfinch, this

suddenly dipping through and rising to sit very still

on top of the nearest pine, big coin, puffed-out,

little hops and hopes when he turns, sometimes

                                 entering into

full sun—becoming yellowest then—these line

                                   endings

branching out too only so far

hoping for the light of another's gaze to pan them,

as the gaze pans for gold in day, a day sometimes overcast,

                                   but what

would the almost-gold (so that I can't

say "golden") bird be but your eye?

Do not harm him. I can bring him back,

and the way he hopped, turning, on the topmost spike

of the pine—how many minutes

ago was it I said "golden"—and does he still linger there

turning chest into and out of the story, hot singular,

not able to shed light off himself yet so

                          full of my

                          glance—me

running on something that cripples me—

do not harm him, do not touch him, don't probe

with the ghost your mind this future as it lays itself out

here, right over the day, straight from the font, and yes

I *am* afraid, and yes my fear is

flicking now from limb to limb, swooping once completely out of

sight—oh flickering long corridor—then

                             back,

the whole wind-sluiced avenued continuum taking

my eye around in it—who could ever hold so many

thoughts in mind—him back now, back, my fear,

and my mind gathering wildly up to still itself on him.

IN/SILENCE

I try to hold my lie in mind.
My thinking one thing while feeling another.
My being forced. Because the truth
is a thing one is not permitted to *say*.
That it is reserved for silence,
a buttress in silence's flyings, its motions
always away from source; that it is re-
served for *going* too, for a deeply
artifactual spidery form, and how it can, gleaming,
yet looking still like mere open air, mere light,
catch in its syntax the necessary sacrifice.
Oh whatever that might be. How for song
I looked today long and hard at a singing bird,
small as my hand, inches from me, seeming
to puff out and hold something within, something that

                      makes

wind ruffle his exterior more—watched
him lift and twist a beak sunlight made burnt-silver
as he tossed it back—not so much to let
anything *out* but more to carve and then to place firmly in the

                      listening space
                      around him

a piece of inwardness: no visible
passaging-through: no inner complication and release:
no passage from an inner place—a mechanism
of strings, bone, hollow
chamber—no native immaterial quiver time turns material—

then towards [by mechanisms ancient and invisible] expression,

and the tragic of all upward motion—

then it all lost in the going aloft with the as yet

unsung—then

the betrayal (into the clear morning air)

of the source of happiness into mere (sung) happiness.

Although there is between the two, just at the break

of silentness, a hovering, almost a penitent

hesitation, an

intake, naked, before any dazzling release

of the unfree into the seeming free, and it seems

it goes elsewhere, and the near (the engine) overruns

into the truly free. This till the last stars be counted?

This plus the mind's insistent coming back and coming back?

This up against that coming back. The death of

uncertainty. The song that falls upon the listener's *eye*,

that seeks the sleek minimum of the meaningless *made*.

Here in the morning light. In matter's massive/muscular/venerable holding-in

of all this flow. Next door the roses flow.

Blood in the hand that reaches for them flows.

PRAYER

Am I still in the near distance
where all things are overlooked
if one just passes by. Do you pass
                        by?
I love the idea of consequence.
Is that itself consequence—(the idea)?
I have known you to be cheap
(as in not willing to pay out the extra
                        length of
blessing, weather, ignorance—all other
[you name them] forms of exodus).
What do I (call) you after all the necessary
                        ritual and protocol
is undertaken? Only-diminished?
Great-and-steady-perishing? Unloosening
                        thirst,
or thirst unloosening ribbony storylines
                        with births
and history's ever-tightening
                        plot
attached? We're in too deep the bluebird
                        perched on
                        the seaweed-colored
limb (fringed with sky as with ever-lightening echoes of
                those selfsame light-struck weeds, those
                seas)

seems to be chattering at me. Too deep?
Someplace that is all speech?
Someplace everything can be said to be

about?
Will we all know if it's blindness, this

way of seeing

when it becomes
apparent? Is there, in fact [who could

tell me

this?] a
we? Where? The distances have everything in their

grip of

in-betweenness.
For better [she said] or for worse [he said]
taking their place alongside the thirst
in line, something vaguely audible about

the silence

(a roar
actually)(your sea at night) but not as
fretful nor as monstrously tender
as the sea wind-driven was

earlier on
in "creation." Oh creation!
What a mood that was. Seeding then dragging-up life and

death in swatches
for us to forage in. Needle, story, knot, the

knot bit off,
the plunging-in of its silvery proposal,

stitch stitch still clicks

the bird still on

its limb, still in the mood, at the very edge

               of the giddy

               woods

through which even this sharpest noon must

                     bleed, ripped into

                     flickering bits.

But it is nothing compared to us

is it, that drip and strobe of the old-world's

                   gold

                       passaging-through,

nothing bending its forwardness, nothing

                     being bent

by it (though the wind, rattling the whole business,

                     would make one think

                 it so). Nothing

compared. And yet it is

there, truly there, in all sizes, that dry

                 creation—

woods, dappling melancholias of singled-out

                     limb-ends, lichened trunk-

                 flanks—shocked

transparencies as if a rumor's just passed

                   through

leaving this trail of inconclusive

                 trembling bits of some

                 momentous story.

Was it true, this time, the rumor?

The wherefore of our being here?

Does it *come* true in the retelling?

                     and truer in

                     the re-

presenting? It looks like laughter as the
wind picks up and the blazing is tossed
from branch to branch, dead bits, live
                              bits,
new growth taking the light less brightly than
the blown-out lightning-strikes. Look:
it is as if you are remembering
                    the day
you were born. The *you*. The newest witness. Bluish then
                                        empurpling then
pink and ready to begin continuing.
Lord of objects. Lord of bleeding and self-
                        expression.
I keep speaking this to you, as if in pity
at the gradual filling of the vacancy
by my very own gaze etcetera. Also the
words—here and here—hoping
this thing—along with all else that
                    wears-out—will
                    do. I think
about you. Yet is only *thinking* omnipresent?
Omniscience, omnipotence: that is all drama.
But omnipresence: time all over the
                    place!
It's like a trance, this time unspooling in
                        this telling.
Like land one suspects must be there, but where?
The ocean kisses every inch of the seeable.
We live. We speak at the horizon. After a
                    while even the
                    timidity

wears off. One speaks. One is not mad.
One lives so long one feels the *noticing*
              in all one sees.
                    Years. Chapters.
Someone is asking for your hand. One turns
                    to speak.
One wishes so one could be interrupted.

II

EVOLUTION

How old are you?

As old as until now.

Under the kelp-bed razorclams turning to find

purchase.

Young things shooting first-times and retaining

precedence.

Razors digging backwards and down,

spurting spittle-bits of sea

to equalize descent.

Do you believe that after you die some part of you

lives on?

Do you pray in hope of reward?

Do you agree or disagree with the following

statement:

it bothers me my life did not turn out as I

expected.

Also there are people on the beach.

And wind accepted by waterfilm.

Look: acceptance has a shape.

And fate—is it accepted by waterfilm?

And how we must promise things.

Do you pray in hope of reward.

Do you pray without hope of reward.

What is it has been gone a long time?

How long is the slightest chance?

Everything in sunlight

improvising backwards,

scratching phrases in a rapid jitter,

where the mind above it begins, ends, tries to get up

                        and move

towards or away from.

You'll feel the so-called music strut hard against

                    the downsuck.

Also someone's shadow going to purchase a beverage.

Also everything in sunlight trying to become bodied by something

                        else,

the whole retreating ocean laying

microscopic and also slightly larger fiercely-lit

kelp in streaks of action—

long sentences with branchlike off-widths indicating

              acceleration brought forth

and left-off, phrases of gigantic backing-off

           from a previously

held shore,

       rivulets of sand left visible in raised inscription

whitening where moistened—questionlike—algebraic—

regarding the long leave-taking—

We are ourselves walking to the right.

The noon hour is itself always a firstness

         of something.

Also, elsewhere, who is hungry?

How small are they? How? I step on parts of

faces, only parts. A whole face, what is that? From here

it seems hard to make out, also a very empty

thing. Like the border of a nationstate.

Being comes into this, idles,

over the interminable logic of

manyness, the demand that *something exist*.

Bending to look close, a

spiking-up and forth of burrowings,

channelings, a turning, a re-turning on

itself where the broad

nouns of large clamshells

flayed open by gulls lie

in punctuating sunlit stillness

on top of a thing which but for

their stillness and expulsion

has no top. The seagulls

hurrying, dragging and retrieving. Also

pecking in place and dropping and

lifting. Sometimes stepping backwards in order to

drag and loosen. Also the drag of the slantline

downtilted towards ocean's sucking further still of

streams of water towards

itself. Of course the future

wasn't there before at all.

This all first time and then again first

     time.

I feel reproach. Eyes closed I touch my face.

My hand hovers like the very question of my face

     over my face.

G says, breathing beside me, that firstness is not, in any case,

a characteristic of experience.

He speaks of the long chain back

to the beginning of "the world" (as he calls it) and then, at last,

     to the great *no*

beginning. I feel the *no* begin.

Subsequence hums tinily all round me,

erasing my tracks. Oh bright/morning. This

                              morning.

Look: what looks like retreating is not exactly so.

Sunlight makes of exactness an issue.

No issuing *forth* of matter

because of sunlight. But sun's

up-sucking also at work. And how

it seems to have weight,

pushing the originally pillowy kelp-beds

down, flattening them where they

give up water, unthickening their

pastures as the tunneling-away from

that gigantic drying drives

the almost-imperceptible downwards:

first glitter then more unchangeable shine slowly being

forced into the vast top of the

beachwide beds. Drying out and

hardening, the beds force light

                              back.

Back across what resides inside.

White closed-in part of gazing-out.

Bothered by the ease of touch.

As if one should open out and spill, again.

Sound in the sun now muted

(is there an inherent good)

as the ruffling back-roar recedes

(is there inherent good in people)—

Sound becoming particular and pricked

with syncopations of singularities—
peeps, insucks, snaps—where light is
                    in domain.
What good is my silence for, what would it hold
                    inside, keeping it free?
Sing says the folding water on stiller water—
one running through where the other's breaking. Sing me
something (the sound of the low wave-breaking)
(the tuning-down where it deposits life-matter on
the uphill of shore)(also the multiplicity
of deepenings and coverings where whiteness rises as a
                         manyness)
(as the wave breaks over its own breaking)
(to rip in unison)(onto its backslide)—
of something sing, and singing, disagree.

GULLS

Those neck-pointing out full bodylength and calling
outwards over the breaking waves.
Those standing in waves and letting them come and
                              go over them.
Those gathering head-down and over some one
                              thing.
Those still out there where motion is
primarily a pulsing from underneath
and the forward-motion so slight they lay
their stillness on its swelling and falling
and let themselves swell, fall…
Sometimes the whole flock rising and running just
as the last film of darkness rises
leaving behind, also rising and falling in
                    tiny upliftings,
almost a mile of white underfeathers, up-turned, white spines
                              gliding over the wet
sand, in gusts, being blown down towards
              the unified inrolling awayness
              of white. All things turning white through
breaking. The long red pointing of lowering sun
going down on (but also streaking in towards) whoever
might be standing at the point-of-view place
from which this watching. This watching being risen
from: as glance: along the red
blurring and swaying water-path:
to the singular redness: the glance a

being-everywhere-risen-from: everywhere

cawing, mewing, cries where a

single bird lifts heavily

just at shoreline, rip where

its wing-tips (both) lap

backwash, feet still in

the wave-drag of it, to coast

on top of its own shadow and then down to not

landing.

*

Also just under the wave a thickening where

sun breaks into two red circles upon the

                    carried frothing—

white and roiling, yes, yet unbreakably red—red pushed (slicked) under

            each wave (tucked) and, although breaking, always

                one—(as if from the back-end-of-distance red)—

and that *one* flowing to here to

slap the red it carries in glisten-sheets

up onto shore and (also as if *onto*)

my feet.

*

[Or onto my feet, then into my eyes] where red turns into "sun" again.

So then it's sun in surf-breaking water: incircling, smearing: mind not

knowing if it's still "wave," breaking on

itself, small glider, or if it's "amidst" (red turning feathery)

or rather "over" (the laciness of foambreak) or just *what*—(among the line of also smearingly reddening terns floating out now

on the feathery backedge of foambroken

looking)—*it is.*

*

The wind swallows my words one

                  by

one. The words leaping too, over their own

                         staying.

Oceanward too, as if being taken

                away

into splash—my clutch of

              words

swaying and stemming from my

              saying, no

echo. No stopping on the temporarily exposed and drying rock

                                     out there

to rub or rest where nothing else

               grows.

And truly swift over the sands.

As if most afraid of being re-

              peated.

Preferring to be dissolved to

              designation,

backglancing stirrings,

wedged-in between unsaying and

              forgetting—

what an enterprise—spoken out by

              me as if

to *still* some last place, place becoming even as I speak
                                unspeakable—
and so punctually—not even burnt
by their crossing through the one great
                    inwardness of
mind, not by the straining to be held (grasped) by my
                          meanings:
"We shall have early fruit
this year" one of the shades along the way
                    calls out,
and "from the beginning" (yet further on). Words: always face-down:
listening falling upon them (as if from
                    above):
listening greedy, able to put them to death,
flinging itself upon them: them open and attached
                  so hard to
                  what they carry:
the only evidence in them of having
                  been.
And yet how they want to see behind themselves—
                  as if there is something
back there, always, behind these rows I
              gnaw the open with—
feeling them rush a bit and crane to see beneath themselves—
and always with such pain, just after emerging—
twisting on their stems to see behind—as if there were a
                          sun
back there they need, as if it's a betrayal,
this single forward-facing: reference: dream of: ad-
                    mission: re

semblance: turning away from the page as if turning to a tryst:

the gazing-straight up at the reader there filled with ultimate

fatigue:

devoted servants: road signs: footprints: you are not alone:

slowly in the listener the prisoners emerge:

slowly in you reader they stand like madmen facing into the wind:

nowhere is there any trace of blood

spilled in the service of kings, or love, or for the sake of honor,

or for some other reason.

DUSK SHORE PRAYER

The creeping revelation of shoreline.

The under-shadowed paisleys scripting wave-edge down-

slope

on the barest inclination, sun making of each

milelong wave-retreat

a golden translucent forward downgoing,

golden sentences writ on clearest moving waters,

moving their meaninglessness on (not *in*) the moving of the

waters

(which feels tugged)(the rows of scripting

      [even though it's a trick] adamant with

self-unfolding)(wanting the eye to catch and take

dominant final-hold, feel the thickest rope of

waterlipped

scripting

to be a producing of a thing that speaks [to whom

one does not know, but a true speech])—to believe this truly,

not in metaphor—

to put it in the blank in which one *sees,*

and then into the blank in which one *is,*

to separate *I am* from *I have being* from *I am*

apart. And not to want to *be*. And never to be

emptied by the wound of meaning.

The gash of likeness. The stump interpretation.

Spelled from the living world. Grown sharper by

this sighting. As sun goes down. Until it glimmers in

the tiny darkness and the human will comes to the end.
Having it go before one's looking goes. The summer
at one's back. The path back barely findable.

THE COMPLEX MECHANISM OF THE BREAK

From here, ten to fourteen rows of folding and branching.

Up close, the laving in overlappings that pool sideways as well as suck back.

Filamentary green-trims where the temporary furthest

coming-forward is lost.

Suctions in three or four different directions back from pinnacle-point.

Encounter of back-suck by the foremost,

low-breaking, upstitching really,

arrivals,

where it seems pebblings of sandbits ruffle-up and are ruffled

back into the foam of

the breakwater browning it.

Glassy meanwhile the frontmost arrivals, their sheets filling momentarily with

sky, with clouds fully formed (in which gulls [of sand] glide) even as they all

are drawn back

into the ruffling front-thunder

into which direct backmotion

feeds—is fed—(over which real rows of low-flying pelicans)—

(backmotion into which retreat itself feeds, slides, you'd have to say dissolves)—

(though strangely nothing of the sea dissolves).

Behind: the crystalline green risings of just-before furling,

then the furling. Between: the wild-carrot lacings and

spume of

breakages the eye hardly caught. Lifting the eyes away one sees

in the near/far distance large upwallings

in which sometimes fish calmly ride sideways

above one,

high above, while close-up, the sky unfolds, deep, here, at our

                                   feet—

(the eyes look down to see up)—(then, squinting, out, to see

                    the see-through slow uprising

                    holding its school). The mind doesn't

want it to break—unease where the heart pushes out—the mind

wants only to keep it coming, yes, sun making the not-yet-breaking crest

                            so gold where the

pelicans turn as they glide—flapping then gliding—

as long as possible without too much dropping—

here and there trying to stay with the just-breaking ridge,

turning towards or away from the

               watching-eye

to origami trick, artichoke wing—sheen—crank—beaks dragging the

gold-fringed, gathered garment-furl through which

              the fish themselves drive (thread)

the only momentarily unbreaking line. And how there is always something

else. Up close four different brown retreating furls just now (being forced

                       to forward-break) re-

entering themselves. Each tripping over each as they are also forced

                       into retreat.

What is force? My love is forced from me as in retreat

from love. My gaze is forced back into me as it retreats

from thought. Sometimes the whole unraveling activity

               for just an instant

pools, all its opposing motions suddenly just pattern on these briefly

lakelike flats—the shore's upslant unspooling then in only two

             dimensions—(close your eyes)—

(although it's only when you open them you hear the seven

               kinds of

sound: hiss-flattenings and poolings-out [sand-suctions in the
                                                            flat],
the pebbled wordlike pulling down and rolling up, the small
hush of the small first-line of white, it lowering its
                                voice as it proceeds
to crash, the crash where the larger one behind is hit and hits
                                the one of yet more force
behind it now, the singleness—[the one loud
thunder-break]—the backmost individual wave,
the lowering and sudden softening of all betweens [of which
every few minutes one] out of which the first crash
yet again can rise. Also the momentary lull: which now lets in
the sound of distance in itself: where your eye might
look up, further out: to where, it seems,
nothing but steady forward progress in its perfect
time occurs: onward, onward: tiny patterns which
seen from above must: it is imagined: perfectly: shine).

EBBTIDE

I am a frequency, current flies through. One has

to ride

the spine.

No peace [of mind][of heart], among the other

frequencies. How often and how hard are answerings.

The surf, receding, leaves successive

hem-line trims of barely raised institching sand—

bridal-wreath puckerings—

glassy (this side), packed smooth (that).

Making one's way one sees the changes.

What took place before one

looked.

Snakeskin of darker sands in with the light.

Slightly more raised and wider alligator-skins.

Crabtracks' wild unfocusings around firm holes.

The single tubefish, dead, long as a snake, half-snout,

rolled over and over as the waves pick up, return, return

less often, go away. For a while he is incandescent

white, then blue, deep green, then white again, until he's

left, half-turned,

eyes sandy till one wave, come back

this far as if in error, cleans him off.

Greenish with rising/falling weed-debris, shoremist

fingering long streaks of sun.

Graphed beachlength on the scallop-edged lapping retreat:

christmas-ornament red shrimp

punctually along the highs of each

upskirting arc—prongs upright,

stiff. Swift ticks of sunlight count them

out.

Who has enough? A little distance

back

two vultures feeding on a pelican. Later, claws and beak

float in the brack. Foam-bits lace-up the edge

of the retreat. Something feels like it's not

coming back. In the tidepool

sand-grains advance along a long

walled avenue, in ranks—at the conjunction of

two rocks, algae

signaling the entry point—(swarming but

swaying in

unison, without advancing) (waiting for

some arrival)

(the channel of them quickening)(the large espousal)(light

beginning now to *touch* what had been only

underwater story)—

until the gleaming flow of particles is finally

set down, is

stilled: the grains

drop down and mat, silt in, begin to dry: the wandering tribe is

gone, the

city's gone, the waiting gone. The individual grains

are not discernible. I'm squatting so I hear

sand sucking water in. Gravity. Glistening.

I take a stick and run it through

the corridor of wilderness.

It fills a bit with water the first time. Is self-erased.

The second time it does not fill. It leaves a

mark where

my stick ran. I make

another (cursive) mark. How easily it bends to cursive, snakes towards

thought.

Looking back

I see the birds eating the bird. The other way my

gaze can barely reach shore-break.

The (little) weight of the stick in my hand. The meditation

place demands. My frequency. This hand, this

sugar-stalk. The cane-fields in the back of us,

the length of tubefish back there too. And

if I write my name. And how mist rounds the headland

till the sea

is gone. One feels word should be sent us

from some source. It is all

roar and cry and suck and snap. The pebbles on the

pebbles roll. One feels one has in custody

what one cannot care for for long. Too much is

asked. Nothing is coming back the way it was.

But one can wait for the next hem, next bride,

next oscillation, comedy. Done, the birds fly

off. I can see through the trees,

through the cane grove, palm grove, out far enough into

the clearing where

the spine of the picked-clean story shines.

HUNGER

(Midday)

"As if twelve princes sat before a king" (Wallace Stevens)

11:54

Thirteen fullest oranges pooling at the foot of

their tree.

In the crater carved-out to contain water at

watering.

Rolled down, touching each other, gleaming.

At watering: heard the early morning

hiss (and deeper

lengthenings)—right in the

birdsound—sometimes

cutting all the way through

as pouring-

forth got

closer. Also heard

the soil in the cool taking the water

in—but can't tell

how to card it [hear it]

out. Now

the eight-foot yucca on its almost-straight

peeling-back

stalk

casting a "perfect" sharp black crown [also halo] on the

ground: right

at its own

foot—so that it grows out of its own reflection—or, no,

out of the reflection of

its blossom-head—the stalk [not

visible in shadow] packed wholly into the eye of the

ground-crown out of which

the actual stem

starts up to *cause*. The cause

(of the crown): yucca leaves

(now in the third dimensional)

traveling out in all the directions, holding the watery sunlight

most in the deepest nesting

center-driven parts of each

individual leaf, but in the widest cases traveling all

the way up to the tip

making white-yellow interlacings of sunbearing fronds twine-up with

utterly darkened ones:

the undersides almost black: me now looking down to see

the crown in its

second dimension (shadow)

move: boy

dragging a bucket at middle distance:

weight in its drag:

me watching the actual crown move in its third.

11:57

Wind-motion: yucca leaves: *shape* moving identically

in both dimensions: wind-motion

only damaging the narrative—(color, relation,

field-to-ground)—in the actual:

the *shadowed* moves with—is—sun—time:

the *actual* told time and time again by sun, a

story, no illusion: a sheet being flapped out

just to the left: behind a

thatched wall: a woman's voice in the sheet—

then snapping—[to shake a dry thing out]—smell of midday in the sheet—[to fold

a dry thing up]—

then song turning to string of words, rising pitch,

11:58

hands gripping, snapping, and so forth (in the invisible):

high laughter—quick—where words,

rushed out like shadow of the song, elicit

11:59

response: then two at once: drone of inevitable unfolding; exfoliating

highs of

11:59

response: above the orange tree's full head of fruit, one

largest-of-all-palms swaying lazily

right through the strongest wind-bursts—

12:00

Everything moving away from core

All patterning being motion-away-from-origin

The limited number of directions a thing can go in

The buzzard above, the furrows of *its* feathers

The circling

Where what one can't look straight-up-at is

Where the yellow hose crossing the dirt yard
makes its circular loop (no shadow)

Where my eye picks it up just as the silence breaks

Where I count six kinds of leaf

hushing and slurring—an engine nearing then
re-disappearing—

[the king down to the one-body-under-the-sun moves, a
caw in the leaf-hissings making itself their core, also
drawing onto them a scale of
relative darkenings, hierarchy hearable as a
drawing of likeness towards its own register, the
blackness of the crow nowhere visible yet fisting
the core].

12:01

The loop in the yellow then the
yellow continuing.

12:01

All the fruit darkening.

12:01

A child whining.

A path when I get to it. The having-moved. The given.

The given sun. The befallen. Why is it the thief gets into heaven.

In this description the layer of thieving.

In all the leaves geometry so adamant.

As if in enough heat the mind is forced inside to

watch: to feel: fear: geometry: rot: math:
light.

(later)

The god: repetition without variant:
its spouse: inevitable necessary variant: its lover: unnecessary
variant: interruption, wall, disease, rot.

(later)

Inevitable
Inanimate

(later)

What can be broken always holding what can [not].
A truth not a symbol. Grip it in scrutiny.

THE TIME BEING

I
(Todos Santos)

Cluster of bird-chatter a knot at the center of a supreme
unfolding. Large river-pebbles almost filling a jar.
Turn it over: where they collide and recollect: that grainy quick
clatterfall: cluster: [of birdsound]: knot.

Near it a browner sound, closer-up, a
single note of it a very thick rope, stiff with age, knotted
to a rusted hinge: in it a higher and a lower pitch (inter-
                              mingling)
(rope squeak and hinge). But that only if the one note (repeated
more or less rapidly)(in clusters of up to five) is singled
out.

Nothing can be singled out.

                              *

We wait for the dog-bark, hearing sun (utterly without
glow in it)(a thing that blanks out into what we call
blindness each thing it washes) in the highest background
lymph-system screeches. Clap of banana leaves, long as a
tall child or marlin. Then the dog-bark to the
far left—for a moment just *itself,*
then the dog-bark drawn in, percussive, in
relation. Then we wait for the first car.

*

Engine rising [we know there's a hill] then evening-out to a
smooth hum, then into the story with fictive
presence, even as it crosses through the length of town then out.
When the woman calls out, it's not as if the netting
caught her. She knots up the far left of
the listening. A small boy suddenly very near to the
right taps a glass jar with a metal
implement, then he taps a different openness.

*

The listening: one is the first of
the fishermen. The net builds. It casts
still further. The trucks on the highway passing town. The
goatbells and cowbells intermingling at the edge of the
canefields. One is first first. Then there is a
portal, saints pass through, light
over all of it without nearing, but shadows
striating our shadows' passing-in, adding-through.
One is first then one is suddenly unable to be
first, it is a strange quick grace. The net
shifts hands, is held at the other side, at the
far side (churchbell for 17 repeats like lower
goatbell)(all sounds always reproducible
[if one rejects name] as something damaged or
frayed or about to break
from wear). One feels sound deepest in the apparently
most worn. In this sunlight, for
instance. Here. Just as I say this and the

[45]

chatter rises in a clump I know not in
response to what. Just here where the
sunlight crosses my sill and the
window-sashes lay firm gray-black marks
aslant the terracotta tiles of floor. Here
where the whiteness of the "vacancy" the palmfronds (full of
transparency and motion) carry back and forth over floortiles' grout-lines—here
where that whitening (wind really) juts wild through

                          all strands of
the netting (sash, grout, palmfrond) and is, of a sudden, made to let up, slow

                                        down, as the

caught fish must.

II

(Palm Beach, Todos Santos)

The whole of the unfolding like a skin
coming-off. Sand striated everywhere by tide-action
packed hard onto it in tiny color variations and
speckling and runs of diamond-pattern where tide
has receded. Monkfish with their porcupine-quilled
tapering backs, all head and side-eyes and quickly
left by the tides. At tide-line, with each
lapping, shrimp left at the greenish fanning wave

                             edge.
Retreat and more retreat. Tiretracks
recriss-crossing the marbled sandskin. Footprints,
birdprints, feathers, broken glass. The fishermen
in the distance on the rocks casting out.
Wallbreaks, the filament where the backwash
breaks and retreats leaving a pooling, white and green,

and also brownish marbled slicknesses [a tiny

stilling, really, in the regrouping of powers] and on

that slickness: filmy slownesses like lung

tissue, or the white netting from

stomach-lining they wrap lamb-kidneys in in the window

display—slightly fatty and good in baking where it

holds the parts together then melts off—

Here melting off: the skin of the

momentary lull where forward and backward

motion are ever so briefly equal—feathery too [so soft] but

mostly marbled [so hard]

yet sloughing snakeskin off with the very next

wave and laying that skin onto shore, at

our feet. In sand: on sand:

palmfronds, feather-layerings: accumulations of differently-gapped nets at

angles not exactly overlapping: drifts of

miniscule dune-structures building like sound-waves

then lowering in sun in fast-moving clouds: making

for the time being, the time being: tide coming back

in and the fishermen now walking this way carrying off

an unusually large catch. The

story that got me here. The breaking waves tossing

spume the whole length of the beach. The glassy

tidal-retreat zone where the reduced

incline allows for a full measure of sky

every eight seconds or so to be strewn over the

otherwise dark-wet sand—a sun, a blueness,

clouds clearly moving, the skin of water

giving us "where-the-earth-opens" [it must open],

sun in there one cannot look at any

more than one can look at the one above—then the retreat—

sun, clouds, blue, all being taken back

into the shorebreak, tossed-up, in-ruffled

airily into huge plumes and upcast mists, the looking-down

leaving tiny holes where clam and crab and tubeworm

suck back under and the water goes *down* as well as *out*

and the earth is filling and the earth is

shut. The time presses.

The sense of one's *person*

numbs as in having been too long in too

strong a wind. The idea won't

hold as I push it out. Then it will. Then it

is held [not by me]. Then it is all gone.

The fishermen seen from the back as they

disappear through the palms.

III

PRAYER
("From Behind Trees")

The branchful of dried leaves blown about at the center
of the road, turning on itself is it a path:
snake: gray-brown updrafting: drama:
whole affair played out between the wind's quiver, wind's
dusty haste, an almost impeccable procedure,
bit of scenery from which all fear
is deleted. So it
is right here, where I am peering, where I am supposed to
                                        discern,
how the new gods walk behind the old gods at the suitable distance.

EXIT WOUND

The apparently sudden appearance of—

                    blossoming-out afresh, out of reach—

aiming for extinction, abandonment—

                    other fossils, then again no fossils—

because of having previously lived on earth,

deviating and branching into use and disuse,

what in it that is transmitted by heredity,

that cannot help the lowest plants and animals—

what is "the lowest," where ends "environment,"

"he was therefore unable to provide a unitary theory of

                    evolution,"

to use reason to arrive at faith,

to bring the sacred into the branchings of the un-

reasonable—the blue between the branches

pulling upwards and away so that branches

                    become

branching, their tips failing at what comes to be called dis-

                    appearance,

as if by too much compromise, straining towards justice till it

                    cannot but

fail. Alongside faith (leaping) always the

                  demon, the

comparative. The presence [only the mind can do

                  this] of

inner feeling up against *living force*,

what exists without having been perfected or made

                  complex,

what exists without having been made,

what exists without having been,
(therefore unable to provide a unitary theory)
(of evolution)(of regret)
what exists inside the sensation of duration—
(inside duration where is the aside to go)(how
far under)(or is it into?)—and then in the aside, the off-
hand, half-formulated, half-heard but yet still
                              living breath of a
thinking, down in the deep station of feeling—
                    though still (barely) out-
lined so as to be [branching] as-
                    certainable
and seizable, so as to be dragged up: there, she
                              thought,
is my thought before me. Like a planted
thing in its pot. Not quite in nature
                    yet still alive
and—most crucially—self-evident.
And that I can feed it. [Yet she was unable still
to provide a unitary theory]. It is
(she thought looking away momentarily)(so that
looking back it could be there more fully in all
its glory: her thought) however small, a
                    catastrophe,
leafing and branching, making of itself a higher
                              and a lower
part, catastrophic, down to its
shadows cast upon the floor,
branchings so still where the leaf-ends
                    sway
in the breeze the curtains have

touched and left off.

Outside, she thought: the point of origin.

They can call it, if they wish, she thought, the

                              supreme

being (blossoming-out afresh)(feeling as if one

had previously lived elsewhere on earth)

(out of reach even of catastrophe)(there had been,

she knew, extensive extinctions) her

                    thinking this now

deep in the *duration* [wanting

so to come back up][but up into what

                    organism of

time][or is it organization of?] the *lasting* of the minutes

                              for example,

the sensation of their being somewhere clocked

                         out in a re-

sistant form, a wage for example attached to

their beginnings and endings, beginnings and endings

                         somehow capable of being

                    exactly

cut off. That not catastrophic, therefore, for

                    example.

Not the organism of catastrophe like a

shaft of light breaking down through the crowning trees

just now [*in* the just now] as she looked out.

And could she be *associated* with it, for example,

                         that instant

of looking-up and light breaking through, could she

be imbricated into the fate [the fate's non-

                    durational

nature for example][even the recess in which

these "for examples" go][always in it, all

                          levels of

                          inwardness—

the progress by the abandonment

of some aspects of creation

                to fate]

[we call this progressionism][but there is

also the correlation of parts][in order

to determine the space to which we, each,

belong][or could it be felt—or thought—

that everything happening now was strictly

connected to something that *happened* in

the past][it was the word "happened" stopped her]

the problem as always was the problem of how

something could come out of nothing.

There was no other question: inside her,

the nothing [she could just feel it] and before her,

[the plant on the table] the something, the thought

of the nothing [for example]. The Creator loomed

                      (as it always happens)

outside, a bit far away, but still filling-in for

the unexpected. She heard the kitchen clock's gears and also the noon

                                        churchbells

on the far hill. She thought of the idea

                of happiness

—where to place that—like a string of

                christmas lights

dropping down into a darkened well

            or tomb [or was it

catacomb]. She saw the images flash on
                    and off
according to the swinging of the lights. *Down there*
                        she thought. She thought
of happiness, the principal part of the
                    thinking of the thing,
its highest part, still reachable from up here by the
mind, she thought, as though a pronounced
                        looking-down,
vertiginous, a squinting, yes, but as if
one species of one's self could look back
                        far enough
(although of course here it was *down*) to
see the previous existent one had been—
the mark of *design* there upon the gap
between them now (the christmas lights)
        (the swaying intermittence of)
(the hiddenness between the frequencies)
(the frequencies)—She felt as if she could
                        reconcile
this present to that one, and that the
                    thinking
wanted that so. And that it strived.

EVOLUTION

One's nakedness is very slow.

One calls to it, one wastes one's sympathy.

Comparison, too, is very slow.

Where is the past?

I sense that we should keep this coming.

Something like joy rivulets along the sand.

I insists that we "go in." We go in.

One cannot keep all of it. What is enough

of it. And *keep?*—I am being swept away—

what is *keep?* A waking good.

Visibility blocking the view.

Although we associate the manifest with kindness.

The way it goes where it goes, slight downslope.

Like the word "suddenly," the incline it causes.

Also the eye's wild joy sucked down the slope the minutes wave

by wave

pack down and slick.

The journey—some journey—visits one.

The journey—some journey—visits me.

Then this downslope once again.

And how it makes what happens

always more heavily

laden, this self only able to sink (albeit also lifting

as in a

sudden draught) into the future. *Our* future. Where everyone

is patient. Where all the sentences come to complete themselves.

Where what wants to be human still won't show

its face.

ESTUARY

She wondered about the year 1000. She
worried the long stretch of horizon's
                         yellow gapping of
sea from sky with an uplifted glance. She
worried its fixity till it wasn't fixed. She
felt the calling herself *she* as the exact
spot she closed her eyes and the whole un-
                         spooled—miles,
beach, mist, spray, outcroppings, current-drawn
nettings of foam that fanned-out in lulls
as if to give the sea a top—oh please—a
resistant stillness on which to scroll—a
flat impenetrability windowlike out onto a
dark that allows only for this reflection,
this side's insistence, to lay itself upon the
glancing pane: foaming scripts, eyes that
follow and follow frantic with indirection. What
is history to this instant between the waves
[she let herself think][although she was really
thinking let me think, let me just think it and it
will still and come forth][and there will be,
                         however invisible to
others, an annunciation][she
put it there again, as if onto the flat foamy
widening between waves, right onto its
hush, the year 1000]. She felt it was a test.
All of this. She heard it hard, that word, *this*.
It seemed to furl-out as from an opening,

a gesture of mind geometric in its widening,

so firm, the this of the visible

and of nothing else. None of the *thinking* she so laid

down hard, the gesture that of the practiced

plasterer spreading the thin gesso

on the church wall, early morning, circa 1000

flat and clean this one arc of his firm

trowel. Now it, the arc, at each degree of its wide math,

can leave the bodies of sleeping saints and move

across the heaven of

the in-front (and sometimes-a-bit-above) visible.

How odd it all is. Was it better when we were

sure, losers of the big game and sure, vision on our heads like

helmets, gleaming, moving downriver, slowly

but surely, excavating new metals as we

went, opening new trees, crafting new weapons of

highest beauty [we were after gold][also of course

in search of slaves][where are they?][also victory]

[what we call saleable value][thirsty] and yet

what is she now that the rimmed gap

between water and sky is empurpling [lay me down

at my lord's right hand][though I am white with

listening (looking) I will not away][lay me

down by my lord's right hand][we are

bloodthirsty, but after legend][after easily

removable booty] strong with gods' consent

[also from our forefathers]. Payment is required.

As I look out [dusk lowering the *she* as well, down,

onto the horizon line, then drawing in, towards singleness, pulling in,

as nets must be pulled in]—so she

looks out, becoming *I*, feeling it to be a

test, counting the lowering pelican squadron

as it rides the goldening crest of one wave, banking

this side then that of it, dipping as low as breaking

allows, fantastic touching-down behind the break, not un-

predictable except by me [and some of us]

[not you]["lord you," but that is love][that

beseeching sound in the core of the self]

also the frigate birds who bank their black and sheer

white scissoring tails [dowsing for wind in

                              priestly strictness]

twelve circling in a cantata now, then a variation left and

right to reconverge [sometimes as raiders

coming upriver for nubile girls or even wives]

[their thanes forced to look on] then banked at the edge of

human peripheral vision, then circling back

above the fishing spot, the break, and just

behind the break, the lull (how can I say

how much is in the lull)[in pursuit of][casual booty]

[casual beauty][(who) had territorial ambitions

carrying downriver towards this mouthing]

[whose value the king could easily

appreciate][song] the notes of the inaudible frigate fugue

regrouping to the gorgeous asymmetries of center,

a prosperity—even duples and triplets in their

line-up, strong-stress and then liquefaction—

a large sum of money being counted

and recounted, a sum being paid in tribute, out of

fear, being recounted again (they part,

grow single, drop, regroup) out of fear,

gold, the watching eye never able to count out

the tribute, unable to get its defense organized,
[everyone on the beach now waiting for the fishing boats]
[what there is is readiness and
waiting][and chance][earlier, near noon, the
man and his son sleeping in the slim shadow the
                              boat casts on
the sand, nestled up against
the blue stripe of boat-bottom, keel,
stray asleep in another pool, ticking of
trucks cooling down—morning-sale long gone—called-out
                              prices—
thrift, need, quickness]
also the-trying-every-angle (from the instant the
                    small-craft touch down)
also dogs lapping, pelicans, seagulls, frigates, one
                    sea lion. She
looked into the dark. I, I. She tried every angle
[the solution to the invader's debilitation
was to try to buy off the raiders]["protection"]
["money"][paying them to go away][gold]
[unearthed by modern archeologists][modern]
am asked to look [she has slimmed so] to where
I cannot quite much longer see. Am asked. By
what. The god now total conquest. Loyalty. We are
where the river spills and sea is all.

KYOTO

Commentary continues, slanting downward.

Ah what am I carrying, what's this load, who's that

out there,

why all this dust? I remember "the oldest of trees."

We drove through it. I "looked." I remember

"all manner of being may swim in my sea."

Slanting upward, tiny bits of rain murmur in my gaze.

Slanting upward, the gaze senses, right *in* the looking—[so

fresh][after

rain, early spring]—the gaze cannot but sense [since

it's not in the

visual field][not at all]—cannot but: the slantline down towards

dis-

appearance. Remember:

the statues you were looking at [in the

old world] row after row in the beautiful garden,

veined-marble after spring rain (so-called), weight placed on the one

leg or the other, as if in gravity, although also actually

in gravity,

arm on a hip, arm holding a

book, a sword, a severed head—a bow, stone quills—some grapes

proferred, long gazing out, long avenues of principles, adorned, with self,

with

representation, naked for the most part, trees just-in-leaf all down

the lanes,

and everywhere *principle,* hidden but manifest, what we have made

link up in the

spine of time [the body of human making]—right there along with the

million grasses waving [in the new world] right there—aspen visible

at medium height on the near slope, just budding out—

ah what am I carrying, what is this on the ground—

or the ocean lying on its side

whispering—or the silkworm-mulberry, the damasks and brocades covering the

globe,

the hush of sateen-foldings over stone, the hiss in the human walk,

in palaces, in dancehalls—or vineyards sloping away near hilltop—

or look down on sea-top, you'll see wind-design—yes—from

here—

[where are we][who's that in the dust?][is there sleeping

anymore]

["whispering": will it always exist]["mirroring": will it always

exist]

[breath on the mirror if you should get so close]

priorities, humilities, imitation, dew-drenching, intellectuality,

[meet near the resting-place][the white-rose wall][equal to][un

equal

to]—so that if [uneasiness in the face of sunset][uneasiness in the face

of sunrise] I ask you now [with unexpected ease]

[with rapid extension of mind, leaping] to come back from

here

to the statues lining the avenue [mind/gaze now darting down it with

a strange foraging hope][as if feeding very quickly and furiously],

ask you to see them blow up: to dust: all "at once": or "one at a time":

down the wide avenue: lining both sides: dawn slowly creeping toward the rim of

visibility: something maybe observing this: from somewhere: the air

soft, warm, known to the bluebird and swallow: then ask you to

rewind [for just][two seconds]

and see [even eyes closed] see this: wings touching then overlapping
each other slowly as the landed bird re-
                    settles. This
I was thinking today: all you can know: then plants and
animals: names of: movements of: your love: your hands: of
when I was ten in Kyoto mother insisting I take
flower-arranging classes: every morning in a city building:
white stone! with many steps up: then a vast room:
acidy smell of fresh-cuttings, thousands: oozing stem-ends:
eyes: hundreds of greens: and
perfumes: and shinings of movement where two hands lift
                    stem-ends:
and color-flash through air to angled-anchorings: said to reveal the
                    truth of *us*: the
four elements: "represented": the harmonies: to give a state of
mind [not pleasure][what is pleasure] what is she
carrying the young woman still bringing the still-wet branches of blossom in
through the small door to the left under her arms: almond and
cherry: changes: not dream not at all that
would be disappearance: who rules this:
more brought in every day: the birds of the finished
                    (your eye's flight around it). See,
you have picked many flowers. You will pick many more.
As for instance in this "thinking" "today" [two blossomheads
there]. There will be flowers forever. This is: Spring, today, April, 2001.
This I am carrying. These branchings, these cuttings. With a whole heart.

The questions:

      What is longest? oldest? truest? plenty?

      Wisdom? Peace? Wavering? Misfortune?

The rules:

One must be blameless.

One must come to loneliness and be lonely.

One must know half from whole.

One must hear the "broken carriage springs" and know them for

the cowbird's unoiled-gate-hinge

song. Nothing is partial. One must know partiality.

She picks it up and puts it down again.

One must see the cowbird spread its tail—just so—and

shut it again, clean, just

after landing. One must know. The rut is the carriage-trail.

Which carriage. The passage through trees—which bird. When.

Feeble sounds. Harsh. Missed perchings. Repetition: its

insistent coolness: me me me me says one bird, nameless,

who has heard what is dead. It's invisible. It must be heard

of.

Invisible bouquet:

[a generation ago][the forests

were][I assemble my books][we plan to]

[formerly][assume the posture][of]

[rushing]   [just a moment ago]

[suddenly]

[breathless with excitement she]

[best not to]

[is different now]

[crown the color of]

[hearing the wild birds in their]

[although it's early morning, I]

[dark forelock combed back, damp]

[days]

SOLITUDE

*

The subject of mutability
Fog   hour   tree   (frogs)
(mourning dove/hiss of train uncoupling)
(inaudible component to operatic sunset)

*

The subject of mutability
Graduation that can be imagined
Graduation that cannot be imagined
(Difference)   (Series)
Appearance out of nowhere of the new
Life-history   Monstrous birth

*

Need that provokes satisfaction of that need.
Account for origin of [such and such]
Change   Undergone
Lust   Hunger   Danger
Cross-fertilize   Maintain vigor
        [protective]
of the significance   of the vestigial
presupposes   a former function
the power of acquiring new parts
attended by new propensities
directed by irritations sensations volitions associations

*

Editor: their possessing the power to continue [to improve?]

      by their own inherent activity,

        delivering those improvements to posterity——?

*

Speaking subject: world without end

*

Animal   Kingdom

Branching   Limbs

(The last branch the branch I'm on)

(The final branching)

*

Had not become extinct

Had been transmuted into living

*

The supposed tendency to perfection

The supposed tendency to increased complexity

The supposed scale of being

The supposed bottom the supposed top

*

ed: allusion to another work

s.s: I do not hold before me the words

    I do not hold before me the words said and under

    stood.

ed: perceiving subject speaking subject thinking subject

s.s: I have to trace a path

    I am sinking into the local the temporal open,

      that other-than-me who is the I

ed: I said: the openness to the world such as we re-

    discover it in ourselves and the perception within life

    intertwine, encroach upon, change to one another

s.s: consciousness seeking to see time and not to measure it

s.s: consciousness that is at once spontaneous and reflected

        [on the same page]

      the look that kills

[my "look"]   [the presence of what is behind my back]

    (self-presence which is not *an absence from oneself*)

      (the figure on the ground)

(it is already the flesh of things that speaks to us of our own

    flesh, and that speaks to us of the flesh of the other)

                *

you must rise   it is said

by anomaly   deviation   branching

from what might have been

the environment interfered

the environment interferes

new needs because of inner feeling

internal   feeling

living   force

out of catastrophe blooms afresh

                *

also extensive   extinction

a new concept of love involving abandonment

creation (of melancholy fate) by supreme being

*

After catastrophe   advance in the complexity
     of superiority   of purpose

*

of the effects   of internal sentiment
of the effects of acts of obliteration
look back   become
[not magnification]   [but change]

*

reformation   realization

*

a part taken away

*

no whole

*

the idea of development enters the world

*

Such is the machinery of perfection: loss
Such is the machinery of history: habit
Such is the sacred theology: history
Trace continuity through recapitulation
Not magnification, but change

*

The eye is adapted to the medium in which
it lives: agency, wisdom, progression, anticipation.
So the idea of development enters into
the world.

*

s.s: Let us therefore consider ourselves installed
among the multitude of things. Let us try to form notions
that would enable us to comprehend what happens
to us there. Our first truth—which prejudges
nothing and cannot be contested—will be that
there is

ed: one is tempted to say, "the things"—

s.s: presence, that "something" is there, and that "someone"
is there. Before coming to the "someone," let us ask first

ed: one is tempted to say "the things"...
Everyone knows apparently what must be

s.s: what the "something" is.

ed: understood by that?

IV

COVENANT

This in an age in which imagination
is no longer all-powerful. Where if you had
to write the whole thing down, you could.
(Imagine: to see the whole thing written down).
Everything but memory abolished.
All the necessary explanations also provided.
A very round place: everyone is doing it.
"It": a *very* round and glad place.
Feeling life come from far way, like a motor approaching.
And in its approach: that moment when it is closest, so loud, as if
not only near you, but *in* you.
And *that* being the place where the sensation of real property
begins. Come. It is going to pass, even though right

                              now

it's very loud, here, alongside, life, life, so glad to be in it,
no?, unprotected, thank you, *exactly* the way I feel.
And you? Lord how close it comes. It has a

                    seeming to it

so bright it is as if it had no core.
It all given over to the outline of seem:
still approaching, blind, open, its continuing *elsewhere* unthinkable as a

                                        gear-shift

                                        at this speed.

Approaching as if with a big question.
No other system but this one and it growing larger.
All at once, as if all the voices now are suddenly one voice.
Ah, it is here now, *the here*. [Love, where is love, can it too

be this thing that simply grows insistently louder]

[It seems impossible it could ever pass *by*][she thought]

this eruption of presentness right here: your veins

[Meanwhile a dream floats in an unvisited field]

[There by the edge of the barn, above the two green-lichened

stones, where for an instant a butterfly color of chicory

flicks, dis-

appears]. How old fashioned: distance: squinting it

into

view. Even further: rocks at year's lowest tide.

The always-underneath excitedly exposed to heat, light, wind, the

being-seen. Who could have known a glance could be

so plastic. Rubbery and pushing-down on all the tiny hissing overbright

greens.

O sweet conversation: protozoa, air: how long have you been speaking?

The engine [of *the most*] is passing *us* now.

At peak: the mesmerization of here, this me here, this me

passing now.

So as to leave *what* behind?

We, who can now be neither wholly here nor disappear?

And to have it come so close and yet not *know* it:

how in time you do *not* move on:

how there is no "other" side:

how the instant is very wide and bright and we cannot

ever

get away with it——the instant——what holds the "know"

[as if gently, friend, as if mesmerized by love of *it*][love of

(not) making sense](tide coming in)(then distance taking

the complexion

of engine

whitely in)(the covenant, the listening, drawing its parameters out
just as it approaches its own unraveling)
the covenant: yes: that there be plenitude, yes,
but only as a simultaneous emptying—of the before, where it came
from—and of the after (the eager place to which it so
"eagerly" goes). Such rigorous logic, that undulating shape
                              we make of
                              our listening
to it: being: being on time: in time: there seeming to be no actual
                                        being:
all of it growing for a time closer and closer—as with a freight
                              of sheer abstract
                              abundance (the motor
sound)(is all) followed by the full selfishness (of such
                    well being) of the being
(so full of innocence) actually (for the instant) here:
I love you: the sky seems nearer: you are my first
                    person:
let no one question this tirelessness of approach:
love big enough to hide the cage:
tell them yourself who you are:
no victory: ever: no *ever*: then what "happens":
you can hear the hum at its most constant: famished: the era:
          love bestowed upon love close-up:
(quick, ask it of heaven now, whatever it was you so
                    wished to
know) the knowing: so final: yet here is the road, the
                    context, ongoingness,
and how it does go on regardless of the strangely sudden coming un-
                              done of

its passing away.

Silence is welcomed without enthusiasm.

Listening standing now like one who removed his hat

out of respect for

the passage.

What comes in the aftermath they tell us is richly

satisfying.

No need to make a story up, for instance.

We have been free now ever since, for instance.

WHERE: THE PERSON

The background, as the car with its music begins

to recede, first reasserting itself through an increasingly un-

differentiated

tick and boom—the baseline's disappearance like one you once loved, one

still waving, you squinting, trying to both see *and* remember—

an urge once "everything" subduing now, down to small-talk, a little chat,

dried flowers staring from a shiny bowl—

then, all round them, increasing: "considerable" distance: the sense of a stranger now

off to

some other business—him *too* now waving—his back the only part you

understand, a stranger's back, receding, of

a certain size, yes, a semi-darkening object, an object of

attention, human. Oh lord what is it. A tent-flap falls. Note

is taken, then note no longer taken, then (what shall we call it)(history) the

massive chitter coming on—(singleness now truly gone)—massive and

more or less (to the human ear) the same pitch and

duration, only this time a serious

proposal, meaning to stick—formal, ruthless, kind, strange, flaring—

then suddenly crawling maggotlike around

a single hammering-sound—succession, more succession—our listening

replacing almost all the silence now, unaware of

division, past differentiation, no single

object but the hammer in the sun behind the fence,

tappings hardening and softening, and always

full hits, after which silence tumbling down as if a birdsong without

song, a mind of space making of itself a wide existence,

nothing else. Wind silks the fronds. They move

their rippling under the harshness of the festival.

Everything seems easily born. All without echo. No souvenir.

Hands everywhere full of nothing, yet very full.

Hard prize feeling hard-won out to the very edges of the visible—

full sun—(a buzz-saw now, just once, then once

again—its rise, quick fall, pushed deep into the chittering—

and then again the chittering poured into seepages and leaks),

(one gust of wind right into it),

(pushing up around the buzz and filling in

                           each emptiness).

Elsewhere things stop. Elsewhere

there is direction and things go along it and then stop.

Elsewhere motions towards good, or depth, or

elsewhere's elsewhere. Here in the hive of sun,

only the toothy present moment lives. Widening its grin.

A broom sweeps off the concrete ledge.

Two phrases spoken by the sweeper as she turns

                           her head.

Listen: between the words, the sweep,

the strands' accumulating hiss, the water dripping from the

upheld hose, low-pressure of the water's fall,

the mingling of the yellow and *the yellowest*: a power, a blind and un-

                                          important

power, but, because capable of being *all*,

still a heroic power. Even un-

vectored, even untrue.

VIA NEGATIVA

Gracious will. Gracious indistinct.

Everything depends on the point where nothing can be said.

From there we can deduce how

from now on nothing will be like.

Here lies: a border then the un-

just. Do I have, for example,

a heart? Does it only *feel* if you make "sense" of me?

Can it, for example, make me "see"?

Can it make me not see?

That we shall never know, of each other now, more.

That there is a no more. Hot and singular.

Surrounded by our first-persons: the no-more.

Before death's obligatory plurality.

But I do know you by heart.

Also know other things by heart.

Interior, spiral, damnation, your name.

What would be the opposite of "you"?

When I "think," it is near the future, just this

                        side of it.

Something I can't conceive of without saying *you*.

The desert is fueled. My desert is fueled.

Daybreak a chaos in which things first come forth

                then mix

as in an oasis, thirsty

for distinguishment.

Then the angels who need bodies to walk in.

Then something breaking light further as in: "it came to

                      pass," or

the way my words, encountered, are canceled,

especially if true, and how they insist on encounter:

finally: in the world: "the impossible": "the little":

"in the house over there": "elsewhere than here":

what is this (erasure)(read on) is it a warning:

omit me: go back out: go back in: say:

no way to go in: go in: measure:

the little fabric vanishes, ascends, descends, vanishes,

say twenty seconds, say wall

(at the same time there is a specific temperature)

(so that eventually the light goes down all the lights go out

together)

(till the level is reached where a fall begins)(more or less

long)

SURF

All day there had been clouds and the expectation
of sun. It could "break through" anytime, they said.
It wouldn't be a large expense, they said.
And can we still use the old materials—
remembrance (bright
patch), the sound of the surf like a laden car pulling out
over gravel, so slowly, in the middle of last night,
headlights kept off, *everywhere* still expected to happen.
She felt the gloom of that architecture:
the plans of the as-yet-unbuilt,
and how sad it was, the young feeling of the middle of the
                                        night,
in it that pulling-away: as if it were really open, the elsewhere: as if
                            we could pull right into it—
the "free" the radio had called it earlier before all stations but the one
went off the air. The surf was also really there.
Behind the gravelly pulling-away into the hope of
manyness: many *kinds* [or will we all
                    be alone
together?], many *outcomes*, many luscious *vacancies*
still happily clothed in the silky "for better or
for worse." Through the windowpanes she thought she saw
things being handled by long white-gloved arms, flowers
placed strategically. The car pulls-out to "have
experiences" [the gravel's motion with like-sound of surf in it, and in it, too,
                            the actual surf
                            beyond]

until—once out the entranceway—the lights snap on and cast
apparently frantic but actually (unfortunately) random

(except for

forwardness)

beams through the woods.

There is, of course,

a place this will

"end up." Even the mind in the house drinking this in

knows this, how the distance can feel "crossed," yes,

how the thinking tracking it quickens,

a kind of laughter, brushing all the carefully-made plans away—

an abrupt exhalation—as if over dust.

Kind people, from time to time, at the edges of

things. Inside, a plain white wall giving one

a feeling of truth. Things waiting in mind to be placed upon it.

Like a cool drink upon it. Things laid on it in such a way

they come to be, finally, *without use.*

Soon *day* again (she thought) you can't just pick up in the middle.

She could hear the surf behind the wind-in-the-trees now that

the car, in its secrecy,

had left [she had heard it turn,

take the two curves and, like small

talk in

the distance,

become distance]. Then wind, the surf, and she was sure

the car was beyond range.

It has *disappeared,* she thought, watching her lit room lay itself into

the surrounding woods,

letting all the deviating paths and openings lead to the un-

relenting surf

"ever receding, ever deferred" she thought, looking at the

                     silk-black panes.

Was she meant to see in? Was she meant to look back in at

                           "our"

selves (room, lamp, sea-green bedspread).

How should she spend this poverty, she thought, looking at the panes

across the room, as if they held some *truth* in the way

                  they faced apparently *in* (reflecting

us) while being actually a facing-*out*. They're re-

presenting each to each [she thought].

She listened over and over as if to *see* by that listening.

She tracked backwards to the last audible bit of tire on

          gravel, listening for the trying-to-get-out-

unheard. It was all still there. And now, louder still, over it,

each wave of surf against which she would play the terms

"happy" "aghast" "uselessness" "perfect"

as if her mind could bend its dowsing wand

into those waves, into those waves' waves, into the foreign part of the "soul"

that was still—(there in each individual break on shore, each rise

                       or fall

                       in pitch)—

what she could call "her" soul.

Is there so much foreign matter in it? Doesn't it *belong* re-

                gardless?

Blurring, yes, but alive with separateness?

To know what is coming she thought, as if to pull day-break on.

That we are moving ... She thought of the car on the highway's

            dangerous and graceful resolutions—

saw its static lights and *speed* as if it were just

          patience—

the escape from "here" a resolute giving-in to patience—
the patience of story—that we are moving
(looking at the mullioned squares of black for story to break
                                in them)(erasing
the room reflected there, in all its parts, again and again)
each pane placing her at a
                        slightly different angle, yes,
[somebody else's car going by terribly fast
                down the main road]
[a conflagration of utmost nearness, appearance and
                        disappearance on either
side] the panes in sets of eight where the window still
                                holds night
[as if something out there is just waiting for you to laugh
out loud][to break][like bending to take the long expected
                        drink of water—
the long "cool" drink of water she thought because of the shiny
                        surface of the panes—
our faces as if hiding in them, in the
room in them, in the surface on the surface that must not
be looked past]. There is no plural of "change" she thought.
Or "thirst."

BY THE WAY

She slept in the wind, she was learning to sleep

in the wind.

This in the old city, late in the season.

For me the world is created [she would think].

Am nothing more than ashes and dust [would think].

The day encircling her sleeping seemed to even *smell* of

truth.

It was committed to using the past.

Thought: what am I supposed to save.

Thought: what am I supposed to remember.

Day was filled as usual with room.

In it the visible, increasingly, its devalued

currency.

All things seemed to be falling

under the rubric of *possessions*. All

things—as if under an invisibly descending mote-filled

mantle—trickling, full of itself—the light beams still straw-colored

holding the motes so gently as they made their way down

over all

things in their luscious but adamant diagonals.

This is where the painters found them, at these

steepnesses—ascent, descent—hovering,

beautiful of

course the

feeling—neither happy nor sad—that pleasantness the

soul (so

gradually filtered down)

throwing away the only world that would have saved them.

Is it possible [thought] to have

experience? Can I see what there is? It was

easier to

ask, for

example "to save one's self is to save what?" But she

(because of the wind perhaps)[it is this wind she thought]

began to feel there was a warning sounding—how

odd it should be so inaudible—as if a stranger from

a long time ago were appearing in a clearing—no, [thought], as

if a

clearing from long ago appeared in the stranger—in it the hissing

what-is-there [was nobody listening?][or even looking]

[and it seems unserious, truly, her throttling this

point][the stranger able to be herself—or *in*

herself]

[not as lovers though, but as a clearing that folds inside itself

body upon body that has

traversed it]

[the whole community][each self

climbing so gently over the next]—the clearing,

with its patches of dappling at the edges and long clear axial

shafts

moving all day around the center,

as a sundial would stir the day but with an element of

stubborn volition,

slant beams tracking prey at the clearing's core.

Meanwhile is one name for the clearing in-

side [at the conductive

inside of] all

the living—lost and unlost. *Distinction* another, as

each soul cards itself from its former and its follower.

All this time they have been waiting.

Then *thinking* (the wind that keeps the clearing open). But not

"thinking" as we

know it. Not to push everything back into the

surrounding

forest. Not to arrive at *finish* at the end.

[The end of what, she thought]

Yes there was life in the surrounding "forest."

Which filled each of the selves to their edges,

hazy with fullness,

restless with hard attention, fruition,

(they were, after all, always all hunting)

(the wind driving the scent sometimes this way some

times that)

(*outcome* the essential love of the edges, of being)—

But once the mind ended, as it were,

a wholly separate mind felt the wind of the

clearing.

There is no foreground in it, for instance, once this is in you, or

you in it—

it surrounds everything like a clear idea—

birds flying up out of its edges, dipping through it perhaps, but

always retreating.

Now you can enter your clearing: dazzling

imagination: eternal-looking with much thistle-down:

wild onion in the notional (hello, goodbye) stroking

of late light:

it grows heavy with emptiness: more wind:

you now in wind (imagine) and this wind in you.

Around you all eras have ended—progress, achievement,

                                        opinion,

the spot where some ruler could be made to stand

exactly, signifying. Even the light-motes seem to say

[exactly]: what is an *explanation?*

People come and go in the clearing digging graves, that's

true. People are buried, slowly, systematically, in every part of it—it

                                        takes

[and yes, at the start it *was* a flower garden]

time. But without the sense of continuity (there are

small butter-colored butterflies) without the sense of

arrangements making up a thought.

More birds fly through. Through the "she" of the

                                beginning

whose clearing this "you" is in. The I stands

                        deepening.

As a fruit ripens. For the summer of the clearing is long

once you enter the first person, bearing out-limbs, carrying

                                        fruit.

There is no looking-back on anything.

The leaves ruffle, restless for the new.

Deeper-in yet, a worried continuing does direct

the passage of time with unnerving ease.

And yes it is important to use your mind to place the

vast analogies of cities all round this readiness.

They have to grindingly cohere

and day come round them, tightening the free.

The circulation of the versions of each instant, too (as the motes

                                do) strengthening

                                the fabric

of the surround.

All is disguised of course.

The sun on the parkbench could be a baby

girl,

the meaning in this tone of voice could be the

meant

or where a century of sleep coheres and sticks—

however momentarily. It is important.

Questions can be asked out here, in the layering

surround—

shedding the versions as a dome sheds each instant

of the given—

as if it were merely too slippery—time—and couldn't stick and so

must pass . . .

The dome of the city: how it seems to rise up out of nothingness

with dawn, and rise into perennial noon, and rise

just this

much further at

the sudden end of noon—an upper story—pulled up by

ropes of

human glance—and shedding, continuously shedding

day. Something grows over it.

Something displaced by its [imagined] rising-up. Something

something fills-in

in the wake of that dis-

placement, yes. Jays overheard now quarrelling, then dropping—

three—

into my shadow, now. Me watching how it's chained to me

as they

hop back and forth, clearing my darkening as if to step

free of a

thought. Hard thought. Free, and then re-

entering. Until the clearing (as if overheard in

                the next room)

(in the voices of others that change

without explanation) rises

again, inside, so near, in the mind, neither in foreground nor in back,

light flowing suddenly more freely there where the edges

                    are, and the clearing

                    itself

is entered—look: there is no one way to go—

light floods a bit, one feels a center, all directions shine from it,

[is a center sought?] I mean, because I'm one of the

few, you know, right here for you,

going on like this, in America,

where the dream is of course gone because it has

too much power, one of the few,

hiding from disbelief,

and it's not a dark place, you know, though so inward,

and it takes up all the room.

V

THE TAKEN-DOWN GOD

(Easter Saturday, Chapel of Maria-Santa)

You are not supposed to write in the presence so I can't really do
this task [*for us*] in there [feel fear when I feel for my pen][in pocket][have
come outside, sit on the steps, people watching me as they
go in][remember]: in there: children who can't see told to kiss a
wooden hand: me watching them feel for it: elongated 18th-century fingers like
washboarded ocean-floor: tide-action grooved-in: mile after mile of the fingers
of the hand of the god, a puppet, larger than life, highly muscled, loose
at the joints, who has been made here [now] to lie down, in our
midst [now], small velvet bed [grave], knee-high to us,
naked, still, of wood, pain [in the face], crown that doesn't come off, thorns
steel, white-gauze wedding veil over the length of him, through which
the small coughs of the weeping seem not
to cross, mosquito netting really—they have made him the bride of
our dirt-waiting, dirt-watching—no—they have whitened the ardent darkening
of his [from which blood trickles] chest, the veil made to seem a great load: our gaze
caught up on it: trawled up in that netting: trawled from the famished
wedding-sea. Oh swim. What are you carrying. You must
jettison it now.

*

Look up, the cross is empty. There are holes on the wall in the
sky where he was, where he will go tomorrow. Usually the children who are
brought will cry. Nervously one puts the money in the little box.
The canopy over him is held by pulleys [gold]. The tassels are made
tremulous by

entrances and exits through the half-open door. And by the coughs or
shushed-up laughs, here and there, of lifted kids. When the bells begin
you can taste the metal on the evening air. It is the only thing
that seems to cross the netting. Iron. Iron as in: women, eyes red, holding
all children still. Look: one runs loose and is not caught in time. The veil is
clenched and ripples where he, in falling, grabs-on, falls, then is picked up
in time, the boy-god's body tilting to one side, thighs wavering, trunk slow, as if
now drifting, now
sinking—how deep the water of the watching is—net sliding off—he seems to
free himself—then all
is rectified.

*

"They gasp." "But one child laughs out loud." "The now." Why are these words
an insult to
the god? Especially if written down. Why this notation on this page a
rip? Presence. Forgive me [I have taken this pad indoors][am sitting in
a tiny pew] I mean to be among the women who surround the god and weep.
They bend and kiss the feet. More coughs. Yes, the speaking subject in
me wants
to rip the veil. Thought "if I bring my pen to bear inside something
will rip." But what? We write. We would like to live somewhere. We wish to
take down
what will continue in all events to rise. We wish to not be erased from the
picture. We wish to picture the erasure. The human earth and its appearance.
The human and its disappearance. What do you think I've been about all this
long time,
half-crazed, pen-in-hand, looking up, looking back down, taking it down,
taking it *all* down. Look it is a burning really. See, the smoke

rises from the altar. And, too, there is the rising that attaches itself to a [veiled] thing: what seems to rise off all sides of the lain-down, hand-made [god]. We

*

would like to say there is *somewhere* from which we are taken to which
                                                    we will be
taken. Ruin, in here, grows sweet. The sweetness seems to rise to cover
everything. I have written in this manner, rapidly, scratching, hearing them hear
this constant incompletion as it tries to *be* (softly as possible) over this page.
Look, they look at me. Some from praying look. The upglance cast
gets into this sentence. Also I hear the chickadees. Also some doves outside.
I exaggerate them. Birdcall against stone wall: etruscan: roman: romanesque:
gothic: birds blistering, up in the archways, finding purchase,
carrying back and forth the bits of twig and something white. From here I'd say
it is a piece of veil—but it was plastic from a shopping bag. We
would like someplace to "live." This appears to you as a photo? This appears to you
as a voice? Bodiless or headless? The shadow of which part of the whole?
Human? The illustration of? A metaphysical impossibility—I can hardly conceive of
you, out there, as I squint you in. Voice and address and attention and in-
attention. Sparkling, in here, the light cracks-down against the walls from
the single, high-up-above-the-altar, window. Like chips of rock, this light
                                              thrown against walls
according to the laws of the broken and the unbroken and
the breaking.

*

The parentlight above this town: curious: one thing: no idea: what virtue
attends it? We value style. No, we are the keepers of a flame called

style. I'm holding it in my right hand. Look—it has such fluency.
The other sounds in here are: currency folded and slid into the little 18th
century box: the cane on the floor clicking in, then later out: the heels of
shoes on stone where the prayer stands in place for a long time: the muttering
where words are cast out into the empty air of the enclosed place:
the whispering which is a different kind of prayer: the sniffling:
birdcries which the open door lets in: the kissing: how the veil
slips and slides over the unmoving beauties of the dead wood boy:
the curious hum of trapped-in light: also more birdcalls: also the call of one
outside trying to find someone: also the second, louder call, trying to catch that one
in time: a name: the (high-pitched) call: unreached, then

reached, a

human attention: and beyond that: the hurrying: the creatures that keep
out of sight: fields, hedgerows, trees: all laying-low their nets of sound
to catch the absence. It

*

is caught. Yes—possession—but of another kind. I promise you. My pen is
a bypath. It has come in from outside. It is colossal, the tiny sound it makes
as I insist in here. How quilled these explanations of absence are as they
group round. Are these sentences full? Are they fresh, as the April air outside
is fresh [near dusk][swallows now beginning to feed]. Thinking appears as
words. "Gli Stati Uniti rifiutano gli accordi di Kyoto—addio
al mondo" [this serves as that which dates the *here*]. Weren't we here? Wasn't I
in here? And you here too? We have "written"—can't you feel it
in your hands [this pen for instance, this scratchy weightlessness] or in your
eyes [the incense filling up this church] or mind ["at the summit of the tiny
hilltop town"]—haven't our eyes the empty cross before them now: here:

*

in this [real time] between us [if you will do the work]: a wall, frescoed,

with fading gold and lesser-yellow trim (pastoral imagery made into

pattern in the trim). And at the center of the emptiness (vertical)(rectangular)

this absence: blue (all over)(no horizon), a brownish empty cross, frescoed wall itself

cut-into in

hundreds of spots, some gouges deep, as if white birds are flying through—swoops,

dips—

long scratches where the arms are taken down and put back up each year—also two

soldiers, weight to one hip: a stance: their looking up at

him [not there]: each leaning on a lance: also two holes

at the far edges of the horizontal plank, large screwjoints where he gets

braced-back, one near the bottom of the vertical, black in those holes where

shadows

pool. There: a picture: the ruin of the mind: did you not *make* it?: because you

can, you

really can: you only have to want to: now

*

a voice will say "Father"—but, no: there is nothing: the

voice will say father meaning by that nothing: now

these words will say "you"—but, no: there is nothing: these

words will say you meaning by that dear nothing: now

this pen will say raise up the man, pull back

the veil, slide it off to the side, meaning by that dear nothing, now

this voice which is called "I" will say to you: now:
now: [can you do *that?*]: now: [do you feel it][there in

your face, in your palms]: *now:* [doesn't it still you][put
birdchatter in][put dusk-wind in olive groves "below"]: now:

we are done we are alone we are a dialect but it can still be
spoken: there is a literal edge: now: there are

facts, too, yes: now: where were we: sliding the veil aside which is
easy, it pulls off with one sweep, it surrenders the body: now

the surround is you: the moment: the [birdcries in it] next
moment and the next: yet now: always still the now: always

still: the body: lift it back up (it will take two of you)
(it is about eight feet): this thought in you: this pen I scour

this church clean with, me on the rickety straw-plaited seat: this
like a full moon preparing to come up in you: all the

tides [raise the globe an instant: the oceans: the *one end* and the *other* of them:
the *center* of: the *bottom* of]: you the litigant

now in this high court: you being asked to argue the case: you: you: now:
strange and low the sensation in you as you lift the slippery wooden

creature

back onto its place, being handed the screwdriver, turning it slowly with your
right hand, left hand holding the center piece (the chest) flat up

against the wall: endless erasure: long calm: long dangerous what-ifs:
and the path: promising both angles: always both: *the* both [*up*

and *down*]

though only *out* once you go out this door.

HIGH TIDE

She held a sign that said Emergency [nothing else].

Handwritten in pencil on the corrugated strip of boxtop.

Everywhere someone's dreams are realized.

Everywhere memory slicks its pebble back and forth at the bottom of
$$\text{its riverbed,}$$

like happiness drifting over what *exists,*

always "close" to its mark—always almost just-within
$$\text{the charmed circle of yes of}$$

what happened—yes.

Over and over the same one spot, drifting near target, recreating the
$$\text{target,}$$

what was it we were talking about, the circle, the circle of our
$$\text{lost}$$

x, forgetting and remembering in the same instant. I came ever closer. I
$$\text{began. I}$$

wrote my name firmly. Extruded meaning—unmistakable

thing.

*

Where was I? It was winter. There where it rolls forward then

stops. The god or gods were not overt. The day [their

habitation] veiled. [Gods disappear at night][One of the

mysteries]. She: a woman of sixty: long gray and

matted hair, many grays, also some blue in it: no light received or
$$\text{fed back by}$$

her skin: and talking all day to the forever-descending in-

visible,

in the dome of listening, in hearing, in the invincible
ministering: talking as if tasting of something on air [frost,
host] and always rocking slightly back and forth—until one is finally

alongside her—

walking by—rags upon rags wrapping her—the whole city's buzzing
code [the one that takes "forever" to transmit] around her,
her rolling and tossing her head, the steam from her lips
lifting blue off her tongue [you can see tongue][sometimes even
back of throat] and growing more silent as I
approach: two women: one holding one word [all caps] up [torn gloves, wool layers
frazzling][moving her eyes as I move away]: then street: then
abstraction of her: then her back there laughing once out loud,
me tossing a quick glance up at the sky, me crossing
the street. I feel scribbled-in. Something inattentive has barely
written me in.

*

Every day I walk by. She is a door with her inscription, I
go by. I look in as if I have nothing to fear, I
walk by. I cross her gaze. We lock in thought, of that I am
sure. Her face cants a bit to peer at me. There is
no identifiable cause and no identifiable
effect. There is no flexibility between hearts. There might be
between minds, I'm not sure. None in the linked-up
gaze. Much in the remembering [gaze on my back
laid hard at first then weakening as I go somewhere I

am due]. All this is in this sentence. Also in
the fractures where periods are placed. You the listener are or are not
expendable, I don't know, I'm not sure. A couple of
days "go by." It seems this could take forever. It seems this
should take Forever into its garb, deep into its folds, and wrap and
wrap it, holding us firm. Firm enough to make
fear not so hurried, there at our faces, there at
our backs.... So I come close to her.
It takes form and time. Who would have expected it
would end this way. The journey out.

*

Once after high-tide along south beach I found a beachlong
scripting
of debris: seaweeds of various thicknesses and drynesses, all
intertwined, some wrappers, shiny, bleached—
strips of mylar, flimsier [translucent] plastic blues—yarn, twine—spines of
strange bits of
fish, and carapaces—parts of birds or were they shells—
actual glass and fishing lures that looked like glass—
all grained-up in the sand and clay that
swirled-up round in ground-winds—nothing extruding—
all woven tight and rolled and braided-up: that's
what I saw hang every morning round her head, but long,
and not just gray but taupes and browns—sometimes some shells,
and always strands that looked like wool. Nearby
her rolled-up sleeping bag and other bags. A liquid thing,
her *here*. Yet also thick. If I get very close,
I feel a wish between us like
a silver thing. Sadness, yes, in our

one gaze [at certain points as you

approach it becomes one][the ends of each long

separation

knit][right there] also the scent of blue [oncoming snow] also

hard snow

already on the ground, also

wonderment also bafflement also still air.

*

Late November, five a.m., walking back from the emergency

room, prescription in hand, ice on the empty trees, I see her

sleeping there, her long thick grouped-up hair over the brick

sidewalk,

the top fold of the sleeping bag flapped back

by strong ground-gusts. Her cheek, exposed,

looks too much more than cold.

I cross the street. Bending, gently as I can, to fold

the blue flap back over the freezing face, wind rattling wildly in my

paper sack, my face blown flat with cold—ache

even in the fingers, even in the eyes—accidentally

I graze her cheek. So far does the mind go, I fill

with the sensation of having

goodness—actual goodness?—fill with my

thinking it good

out to the very edges of my hand—touching her cheek—feel love?: it's not

a cheek, it's paste—or gum and some admixture—

pull the hair back and it's not hair, it's wool and phloxed-up

random yarns, old woolen caps stuffed in a stocking

face, with gum laid on—or is it latex paint—onto

the cheek, making a chin: it is a puppet: it is a place

holding a place: it is an eclipse of: of holding
on: of *on*: or *in*: or what a *here* can be
                    if what one is

is finally reduced to *here*: it is *not* "now": that's what's

been taken elsewhere now: strange splitting of this
atom: her in my mind as it bends down to

feel along: a seam in mesh near where the ear
would be: but running down the front, no mouth, no

hole—I seek a rip—a mark, a stitching-in—if only for the trickery—

moving back up it's only crusted lacquer tells me
it is eyes—I feel with fingertip and it flakes off, what must be

pupil painted on: must find the words: no:
must find what sparkles here, what virtue is existing

only here: my self: her self: this holding-of-place: this strict
                    eight feet of
sidewalk in America: America: you witch: dreaming always of here from an

elsewhere, from a nowhere: I'm looking through a wind that's like a wall for
a proper name: for identification: representation:

divine emptiness: it's been 21 minutes:
crashing, the wave deposits its gift: difference: indifference:

and the long sepulcher: identity: open: *meanwhile* in the arms of
elsewhere: someone has pushed the rock aside: I see

the loan: I see its terms (maybe): I see the payable and
the unpayable: the open-ended credit: created: equal: look.

RELAY STATION

There is [in truth] a highest tide each year—
yes—there are many things—words that come *and* go—

things that are *kept*—[these all high tides]—or where there is
                                        [as if]
a partly open door [of sorts] through which some of
                                the residue of

origin can, broken off from source, ride, just a little higher, deeper,
                                                deeper-in,

in-through. In truth, there is, in grammar,

something where one is truly *one*—link by link,
crystalline—

into which [through which] the voice can empty and refract
what has been seen, or thought, or thought to have been seen,

or to have been. Sometimes one's hopes are "realized."
Sometimes, just before the highest tide's one, single, highest wave
                                        retreats,

a thing and its description *can* be one: can be *the time it takes to say the*
thing. The thing. Laid right down there in "the word," down, as a weight in
                                                its weight,

down—[lord as if garnished with laurel]—[more on that later but
                                for now

this]—until here it is: the cargo: [arrival][stressful][yes][as any singleness is][a
                                                            star][a

bird][a caught thing in a web just now ceasing to stir]—laid
down as the abstract-sense is laid onto the thing—[not as these actual bees

covering this hill, but as the *hum*][an ache over the thing][the rising and
                                        slightly enlarging
                                        change of its
nature][formal][it was going to take

forever][words the first act][such a liquid thing the first act]["the point"]

[the correctness of it]—then *eternity!* How one expected, rising and
                                        lowering with
these tides, for it to keep making its cameo appearance: what one saw from

the suddenly uplifted rise of a wavetop, for instance: quick: through: not like
a dream no: not even fever no: even from here knowing it to be painstaking: e-
                                        laborated:

directing everything forward onto shoreline, expectant, never anything but
                                        expectant,
pushed forever from behind.

NOTES

PRAYER ("minnows") was written as a turn-of-the-millennium poem for the *New York Times* Op-Ed page, and was originally dated 12.31.00

EVOLUTION ("How old are you?"): some of the questions were provided by the questionnaire the *New York Times* used in conducting the poll the results of which were given me as an "assignment" for this poem. An additional fact, which reached me while I was writing this poem, struck me: during the 1850s, while Darwin was concluding *On the Origin of Species*, the rate of extinction [for species] is believed to have been one every five years. Today, the rate of extinction is estimated at one every nine minutes. Throughout the writing of this book, I was haunted by the sensation of that nine-minute span—which might amount to the time it takes to read any poem here before you. My sense of that time frame [and its inevitable increase, even as we "speak"] inhabits, as well as structures, the book. It is written up against the sensation of what is now called "ecocide." I was also influenced by, among other texts, the "World Scientists' Warning to Humanity," sponsored by the Union of Concerned Scientists (1993).

PRAYER ("From Behind Trees"): the last line is loosely based on a line of Zbigniew Herbert's in his prose-poem "Cernunnos" (from *Elegy for the Departure*). I take my poem to be in conversation with such notion of the gods—and of how history transforms them—as is put forth in Herbert's poem. In attempting to enact a realistic description of metamorphoses, "Prayer" wonders, among other things, what the "suitable" distance between subject and object, gods and humans, humans and nature, might indeed be.

ESTUARY: some parenthetical fragments of facts are taken from *The Year 1000: What Life Was Like at the Time of the First Millennium* by Robert Lacey (Danny Danziger, 1999).

KYOTO owes a debt to Gary Snyder in its second and third line, and is dedicated to him.

SOLITUDE: some language—especially individual terms—is taken from Darwin, using the Norton Critical Edition, selected and edited by Philip Appleman, as well as from Merleau Ponty's *The Visible and the Invisible* (Alphonso Lingis, translator, Northwestern University Press, 1968).

THE TAKEN-DOWN GOD: the tiny church in Umbria, Italy, where this takes place is not given its actual name in the subtitle. The phrase in the sixth section, taken from an Italian newspaper headline, translates as "The United States refuses the Kyoto Accords—farewell to the world."

ABOUT THE AUTHOR

Jorie Graham is author of eight collections of poetry, including *The Dream of the Unified Field: Selected Poems 1974–1994,* which won the Pulitzer Prize. She lives in Cambridge, Massachusetts, and teaches at Harvard University.